Audio and MIDI
Access Included

BOOK TWO 2

POPULAR PIANO SOLOS

JOHN THOMPSON'S
ADULT PIANO COURSE

The price of this publication includes access to audio and MIDI tracks online
for download or streaming, using the unique code below.

To access audio visit:
www.halleonard.com/mylibrary

6045-7362-1564-8481

ISBN 978-1-4803-6746-3

EXCLUSIVELY DISTRIBUTED BY

WM WILLIS MUSIC

HAL•LEONARD®
CORPORATION
7777 W. BLUEMOUND RD. P.O. BOX 13819
MILWAUKEE, WISCONSIN 53213

Visit Hal Leonard Online at
www.halleonard.com

The popular songs in this collection were arranged and edited with the adult student in mind. They are perfectly suited to the student learning from *John Thompson's Adult Piano Course* (Book 2), but are also appropriate for students learning from any method, or for anyone playing the piano for personal pleasure and enjoyment.

CONTENTS

Sway
(Quién Será)

With *John Thompson's Adult
Piano Course (Book 2),* use
after page 7.

English Words by Norman Gimbel
Spanish Words and Music by Pablo Beltrán Ruiz
Arranged by Eric Baumgartner

With energy

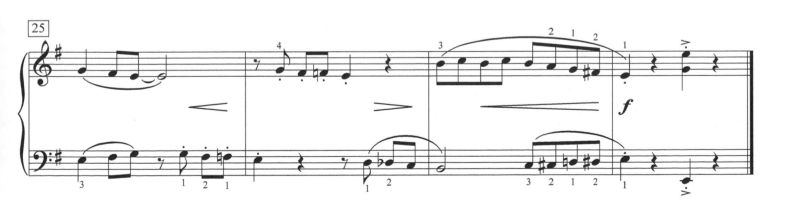

And So It Goes

Use after page 16.

Words and Music by Billy Joel
Arranged by Eric Baumgartner

Wistful, with rubato

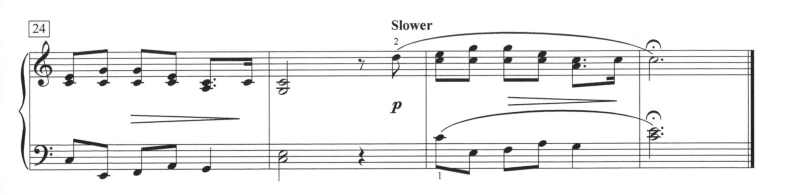

Nadia's Theme
from THE YOUNG AND THE RESTLESS

Use after page 23.

By Barry DeVorzon and Perry Botkin, Jr.
Arranged by Eric Baumgartner

Moderately, with expression

Hey Jude

Use after page 25.

Words and Music by John Lennon
and Paul McCartney
Arranged by Eric Baumgartner

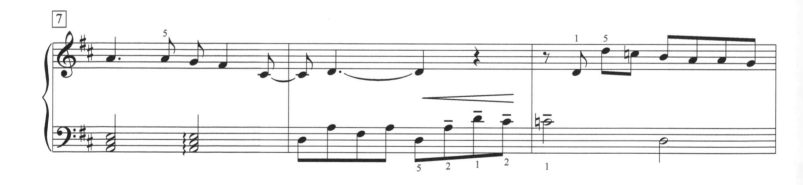

Getting to Know You

from THE KING AND I

Use after page 27.

Lyrics by Oscar Hammerstein II
Music by Richard Rodgers
Arranged by Glenda Austin

Lightly, with a lilt

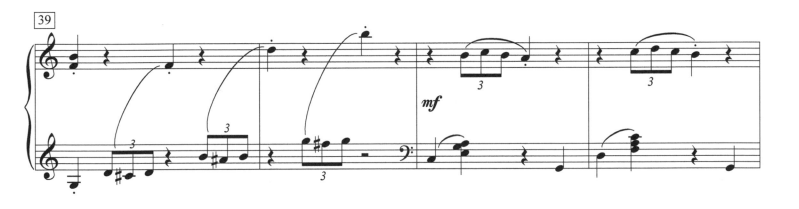

Beauty and the Beast
from Walt Disney's BEAUTY AND THE BEAST

Use after page 37.

Lyrics by Howard Ashman
Music by Alan Menken
Arranged by Glenda Austin

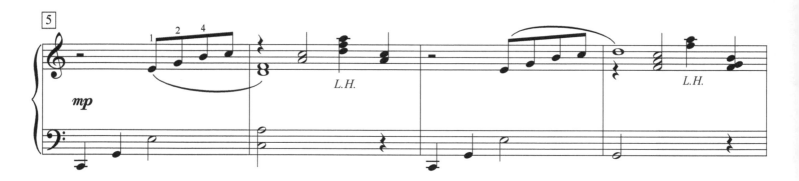

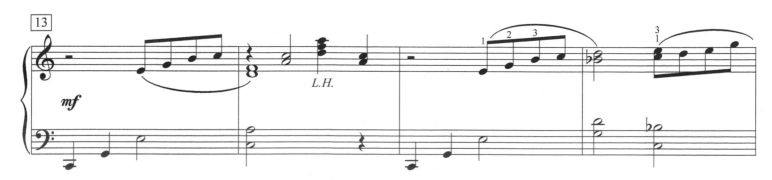

If My Friends Could See Me Now
from SWEET CHARITY

Use after page 41.

Music by Cy Coleman
Lyrics by Dorothy Fields
Arranged by Eric Baumgartner

Moderately bright

My Favorite Things

from THE SOUND OF MUSIC

Lyrics by Oscar Hammerstein II
Music by Richard Rodgers
Arranged by Glenda Austin

Use after page 57.

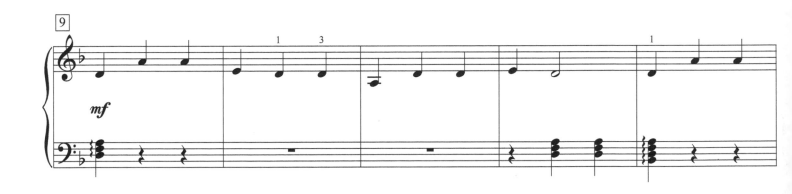

Lollipop

Use after page 67.

Words and Music by Beverly Ross
and Julius Dixon
Arranged by Eric Baumgartner

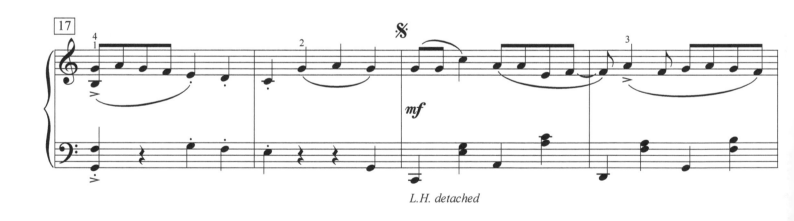

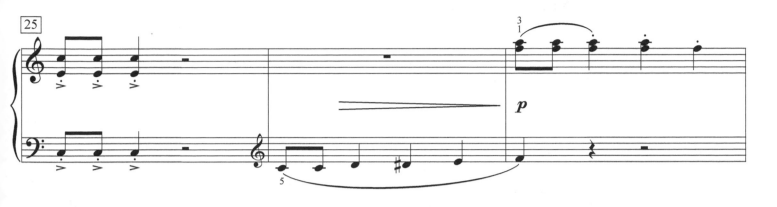

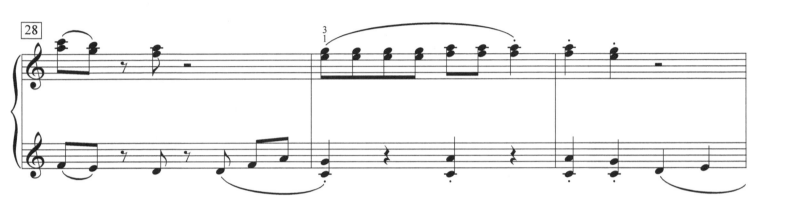

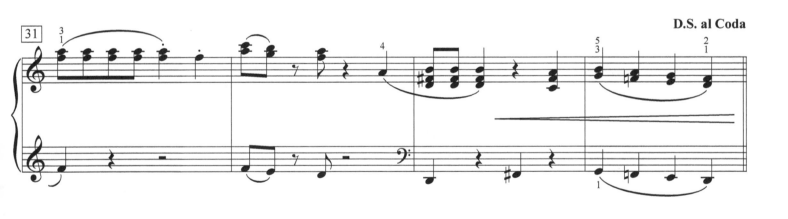

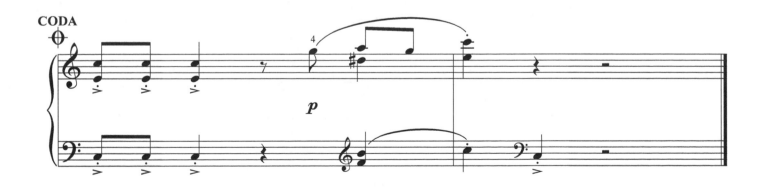

Strawberry Fields Forever

Use after page 71.

Words and Music by John Lennon
and Paul McCartney
Arranged by Eric Baumgartner

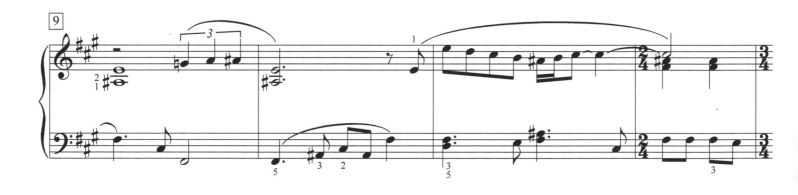

Sunrise, Sunset
from the Musical FIDDLER ON THE ROOF

Use after page 75.

Words by Sheldon Harnick
Music by Jerry Bock
Arranged by Eric Baumgartner

Graceful Waltz tempo

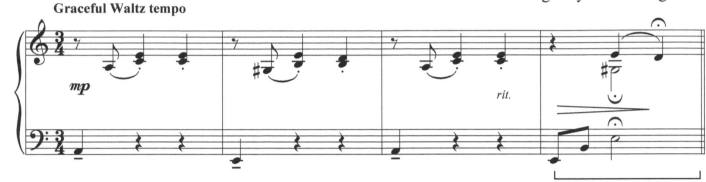

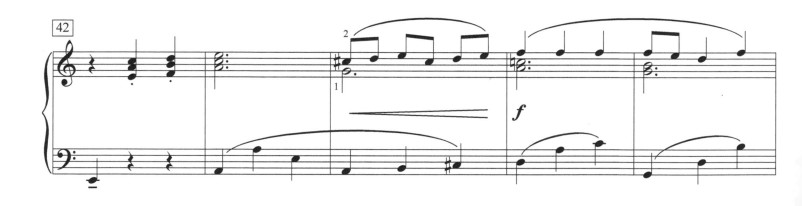

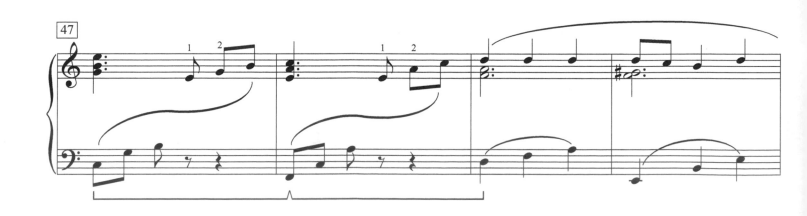

You Raise Me Up

Use after page 82.

Words and Music by Brendan Graham
and Rolf Lovland
Arranged by Eric Baumgartner

COMPOSER'S CHOICE

The Composer's Choice series showcases piano works by an exclusive group of composers, all of whom are also teachers and performers. Each collection contains 8 original solos and includes classic piano pieces that were carefully chosen by the composer, as well as brand-new compositions written especially for the series. The composers also contributed helpful and valuable performance notes for each collection. Get to know a new Willis composer today!

CLOSER LOOK

View sample pages and hear audio excerpts online at
www.halleonard.com

 @WillisPianoMusic

 willispiano

 @WillisPiano

 Willis Piano Music

WILLIS MUSIC

EXCLUSIVELY DISTRIBUTED BY

HAL•LEONARD®
www.willispianomusic.com

Prices, contents, and availability subject to change without notice.

ELEMENTARY

GLENDA AUSTIN
MID TO LATER ELEMENTARY
Betcha-Can Boogie • Jivin' Around • The Plucky Penguin • Rolling Clouds • Shadow Tag • Southpaw Swing • Sunset Over the Sea • Tarantella (Spider at Midnight).
00130168 ....$6.99

CAROLYN MILLER
MID TO LATER ELEMENTARY
The Goldfish Pool • March of the Gnomes • More Fireflies • Morning Dew • Ping Pong • The Piper's Dance • Razz-a-ma-tazz • Rolling River.
00118951 ....$7.99

CAROLYN C. SETLIFF
EARLY TO LATER ELEMENTARY
Dark and Stormy Night • Dreamland • Fantastic Fingers • Peanut Brittle • Six Silly Geese • Snickerdoodle • Roses in Twilight • Seahorse Serenade.
00119289 ....$7.99

INTERMEDIATE

GLENDA AUSTIN
EARLY TO MID-INTERMEDIATE
Blue Mood Waltz • Chromatic Conversation • Etude in E Major • Midnight Caravan • Reverie • South Sea Lullaby • Tangorific • Valse Belle.
00115242 ....$9.99

ERIC BAUMGARTNER
EARLY TO MID-INTERMEDIATE
Aretta's Rhumba • Beale Street Boogie • The Cuckoo • Goblin Dance • Jackrabbit Ramble • Journey's End • New Orleans Nocturne • Scherzando.
00114465 ....$9.99

RANDALL HARTSELL
EARLY TO MID-INTERMEDIATE
Above the Clouds • Autumn Reverie • Raiders in the Night • River Dance • Showers at Daybreak • Sunbursts in the Rain • Sunset in Madrid • Tides of Tahiti.
00122211 ....$8.99

NAOKO IKEDA
EARLY TO MID-INTERMEDIATE
Arigato • The Glacial Mermaid • Land of the Midnight Sun • Sakura • Scarlet Hearts (solo version) • Shooting Stars in Summer • Soft Rain (Azisai) • ...You.
00288891 ....$8.99

CAROLYN MILLER
EARLY INTERMEDIATE
Allison's Song • Little Waltz in E Minor • Reflections • Ripples in the Water • Arpeggio Waltz • Trumpet in the Night • Toccata Semplice • Rhapsody in A Minor.
00123897 ....$8.99

CLASSIC PIANO REPERTOIRE

e *Classic Piano Repertoire* series includes popular as well as lesser-known pieces from a select group of composers
t of the Willis piano archives. Every piece has been newly engraved and edited with the aim to preserve each
mposer's original intent and musical purpose.

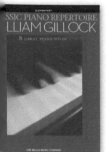

WILLIAM GILLOCK - ELEMENTARY

8 Great Piano Solos

Dance in Ancient Style • Little Flower Girl of Paris • On a Paris Boulevard • Rocking Chair Blues • Sliding in the Snow • Spooky Footsteps • A Stately Sarabande • Stormy Weather.

00416957 ....$8.99

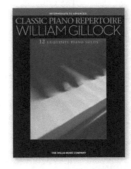

WILLIAM GILLOCK - INTERMEDIATE TO ADVANCED

12 Exquisite Piano Solos

Classic Carnival • Etude in A Major (The Coral Sea) • Etude in E Minor • Etude in G Major (Toboggan Ride) • Festive Piece • A Memory of Vienna • Nocturne • Polynesian Nocturne • Sonatina in Classic Style • Sonatine • Sunset • Valse Etude.

00416912 .... $12.99

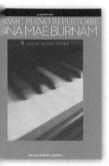

EDNA MAE BURNAM - ELEMENTARY

8 Great Piano Solos

The Clock That Stopped • The Friendly Spider • A Haunted House • New Shoes • The Ride of Paul Revere • The Singing Cello • The Singing Mermaid • Two Birds in a Tree.

00110228 ....$8.99

EDNA MAE BURNAM - INTERMEDIATE TO ADVANCED

13 Memorable Piano Solos

Butterfly Time • Echoes of Gypsies • Hawaiian Leis • Jubilee! • Longing for Scotland • Lovely Senorita • The Mighty Amazon River • Rumbling Rumba • The Singing Fountain • Song of the Prairie • Storm in the Night • Tempo Tarantelle • The White Cliffs of Dover.

00110229 .... $12.99

JOHN THOMPSON - ELEMENTARY

9 Great Piano Solos

Captain Kidd • Drowsy Moon • Dutch Dance • Forest Dawn • Humoresque • Southern Shuffle • Tiptoe • Toy Ships • Up in the Air.

00111968 ....$8.99

JOHN THOMPSON - INTERMEDIATE TO ADVANCED

12 Masterful Piano Solos

Andantino (from Concerto in D Minor) • The Coquette • The Faun • The Juggler • Lagoon • Lofty Peaks • Nocturne • Rhapsody Hongroise • Scherzando in G Major • Tango Carioca • Valse Burlesque • Valse Chromatique.

00111969 .... $12.99

LYNN FREEMAN OLSON - EARLY TO LATER ELEMENTARY

14 Great Piano Solos

Caravan • Carillon • Come Out! Come Out! (Wherever You Are) • Halloween Dance • Johnny, Get Your Hair Cut! • Jumping the Hurdles • Monkey on a Stick • Peter the Pumpkin Eater • Pony Running Free • Silent Shadows • The Sunshine Song • Tall Pagoda • Tubas and Trumpets • Winter's Chocolatier.

0294722 ....$9.99

LYNN FREEMAN OLSON - EARLY TO MID-INTERMEDIATE

13 Distinctive Piano Solos

Band Wagon • Brazilian Holiday • Cloud Paintings • Fanfare • The Flying Ship • Heroic Event • In 1492 • Italian Street Singer • Mexican Serenade • Pageant Dance • Rather Blue • Theme and Variations • Whirlwind.

00294720 ....$9.99

CLOSER LOOK View sample pages and hear audio excerpts online at **www.halleonard.com**

www.willispianomusic.com

 www.facebook.com/willispianomusic

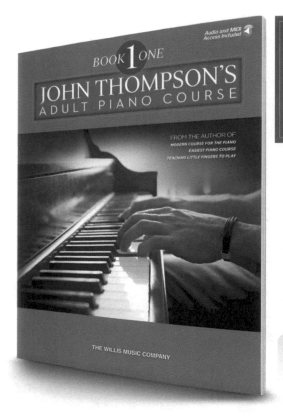

REDISCOVER
JOHN THOMPSON'S
ADULT PIANO COURSE

ADULT PIANO COURSE
Recently re-engraved and updated, *John Thompson's Adult Piano Course* was compiled with the mature student in mind. Adults have the same musical road to travel as the younger student, but the study material for mature students will differ slightly in content. Since these beloved books were written and arranged especially for adults, they contain a wonderful mix of classical arrangements, well-known folk-tunes and outstanding originals that many will find a pleasure to learn and play. Most importantly, the student is always encouraged to play as artistically and with as much musical understanding as possible. Access to orchestrations online is available and features two tracks for each piece: a demo track with the piano part, and one with just the accompaniment.

00122297	Book 1 – Book/Online Audio	$14.99
00412639	Book 1 – Book Only	$6.99
00122300	Book 2 – Book/Online Audio	$14.99
00415763	Book 2 – Book Only	$6.99

POPULAR PIANO SOLOS – JOHN THOMPSON'S ADULT PIANO COURSE
12 great arrangements that can be used on their own, or as a supplement to *John Thompson's Adult Piano Course*.
Each book includes access to audio tracks online that be downloaded or streamed.

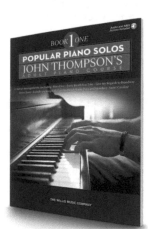

BOOK 1
arr. Carolyn Miller
Born Free • Can't Help Falling in Love • Every Breath You Take • Fields of Gold • Give My Regards to Broadway • A Groovy Kind of Love • My Life • Ob-La-Di, Ob-La-Da • Open Arms • Raindrops Keep Fallin' on My Head • Rainy Days and Mondays • Sweet Caroline.

00124215 Book/Online Audio $12.99

BOOK 2
arr. Eric Baumgartner & Glenda Austin
And So It Goes • Beauty and the Beast • Getting to Know You • Hey Jude • If My Friends Could See Me Now • Lollipop • My Favorite Things • Nadia's Theme • Strawberry Fields Forever • Sunrise, Sunset • Sway (Quien Será) • You Raise Me Up.

00124216 Book/Online Audio $12.99

Also Available, **JOHN THOMPSON RECITAL SERIES**:

SPIRITUALS
Intermediate to Advanced Level
Six excellent arrangements that are ideal for recital or church service. Titles: Deep River • Heav'n, Heav'n • I Want to Be Ready (Walk in Jerusalem, Jus' like John) • Nobody Knows De Trouble I've Seen • Short'nin' Bread • Swing Low, Sweet Chariot.

00137218 .... $6.99

THEME AND VARIATIONS
Intermediate to Advanced Level
Fantastic recital variations that are sure to impress: Chopsticks • Variations on Mary Had a Little Lamb • Variations on Chopin's C Minor Prelude • Three Blind Mice - Variations on the Theme • Variations on Twinkle, Twinkle, Little Star.

00137219.............................. $8.99

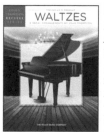

WALTZES
Intermediate to Advanced Level
Excellent, virtuosic arrangements of famous romantic wáltzes: Artist's Life (Strauss) • Paraphrase on the Beautiful Blue Danube (Strauss) • Dark Eyes (Russian Cabaret Song) • Vienna Life (Strauss) • Waltz of the Flowers (Tchaikovsky) • Wedding of the Winds (John T. Hall).

00137220.............................. $8.99

Prices, contents, and availability subject to change without notice.

Please visit www.willispianomusic.com for these and hundreds of other classic and new publications from Willis Music.

EXCLUSIVELY DISTRIBUTED BY